102002

j919.8 Tolboom, Wanda (Neill)
  Tol   People of the snow; the challenge of
         Eskimo Canada. Maps by Donald Pitcher.
         New York, Coward McCann, 1956.
            96 p. illus. maps. (Challenge books,
         eye witness reports)

RELATED
BOOKS IN   1. Eskimos – Canada. I. Title.
CATALOG   mj
UNDER   11069

For hundreds of years Eskimos have managed to survive in one of the coldest, bitterest, most barren lands in the world. Here under the glimmer of the northern lights they build their houses of snow and hunt the caribou and the seal.

Kudluk, Noona, and their son belong to a camp of some thirty Eskimos who move from one site to another in search of food. When Kudluk tracks down a polar bear or caribou, the entire camp feasts; and when his wife begins the task of stretching, drying, cutting, and sewing the skin, the other women help her. As Noona works, her son rests in the hood of her parka, still too young to follow Kudluk on dog-sled journeys, to stalk small animals, or to build play igloos.

In their daily fight for life, the Eskimos find shelter, heat, food, and clothing where there appear to be only wild animals, rocks, and snow. A new challenge has come from the growth of air transport, as men have flown north with new ideas and techniques to establish a safety net of radar outposts across Northern Canada.

Information Office, Canadian Consulate General

People of the Snow

THE CHALLENGE OF ESKIMO CANADA

by Wanda Tolboom

MAPS BY DONALD PITCHER

Coward-McCann, Inc., New York

Contents

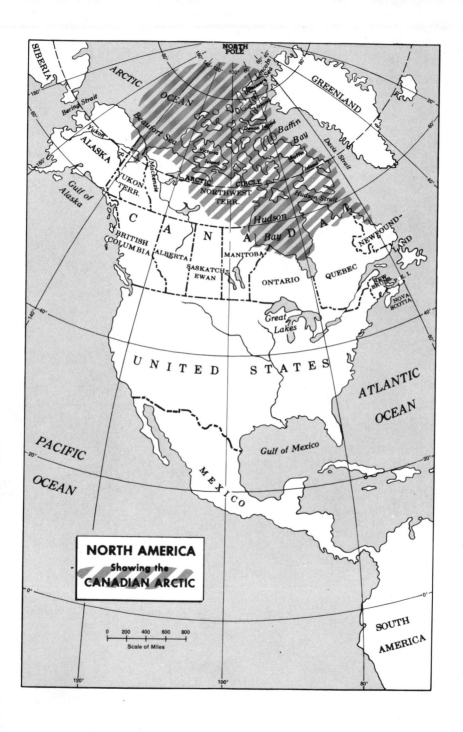

NORTH AMERICA
Showing the
CANADIAN ARCTIC

About This Book

FAR BEYOND the fringe of civilization lies a frozen land known as the Canadian Arctic. Wind-swept and lonely, it stretches for a million square miles across the northernmost part of the Americas. It is a silent and often cruel land of barren hills and plains where no trees grow and only jagged rocks point upward toward the sky. Here snow lies almost all year round. Here winter gales sweep down from the North Pole, turning even the raging seas to ice.

Yet across this great white land roam living creatures —and a race of people who dwell in houses made of snow. These people are the Eskimos.

The Eskimos call themselves the Innuit, which means the People. They dislike the word *Eskimo*, which came originally from the Indian language and means "eaters of raw meat." This name was first given to them scornfully by their southern neighbors, the Canadian Indians. Later it came into general use, but today's Eskimos still proudly prefer to be known as the People. And they are truly the People of the Snow.

Their land stretches across northern Canada from Alaska to Greenland. In the west it is low, with wide plains and rolling hills. Farther east it is rugged, with high mountains and deep valleys. The far north is desolate—large islands covered with ice-capped mountains.

An Eskimo hunter sights across the ice, looking for seals.

National Film Board of Canada

Only about twelve thousand Eskimos live in this sprawling land. They dwell mostly along the coasts. Recently a few families have ventured into the north, where game is more plentiful. But there the extreme cold and almost continual darkness of winter are disliked by even the hardiest Eskimo. That is why most of the People live to the south.

The western Eskimos are fewer in number. More than 75 per cent of the total Eskimo population lives in the east. Here dwell a soft-spoken smiling people whose camps are scattered in greatest numbers along the coasts of northern Quebec and Labrador, Baffin Island, Southampton Island, and that part of the Canadian mainland which lies northwest of Hudson Bay. These Eskimos live mainly on seal. They trap white foxes and sell the skins at the nearest trading post, where they can purchase all manner of goods in return. But at the same time they manage to keep their old way of life.

This book is about the People of the east. In part, it is the story of Kudluk, an Eskimo hunter, his daily life, and the lives of his family and friends. But above all, this is the story of how the Eskimos survive the bitter elements of their barren land by refusing to fight them, quietly accepting and using these elements for their own benefit.

This is the story of the brave and clever Innuit—the People of the Snow.

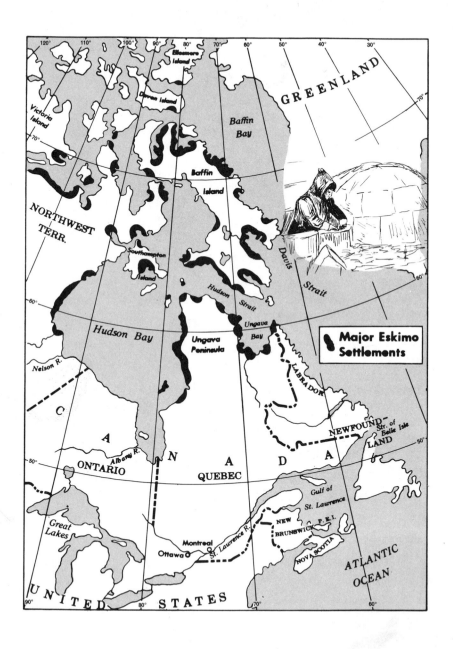

120° 110° 100° 90° 80° 70° 60° 50° 40° 30°

Ellesmere
Island

Devon Island

GREENLAND

70°

Victoria
Island

Baffin
Bay

70°

Baffin

NORTHWEST
TERR.

Island

Southampton
Island

Davis

60°

Hudson

Strait

Strait

60°

Hudson Bay

Ungava
Peninsula

Ungava
Bay

Major Eskimo
Settlements

Nelson R.

LABRADOR

C

A

Albany R.

NEWFOUND-
LAND

Str. of
Belle Isle

50°

ONTARIO

N

A

D

A

50°

QUEBEC

Gulf of
St. Lawrence

Great
Lakes

Montreal

NEW
BRUNSWICK

P.E.I.

Ottawa

St. Lawrence R.

NOVA SCOTIA

ATLANTIC
OCEAN

UNITED

STATES

70°

60°

90°

80°

1. The Land and the Coming of the People

ON A STRETCH of rough ice, not far from the shore of the Arctic sea, a polar bear lumbers on his way. The big white beast does not hurry. Behind him he has left the carcass of a half-eaten seal. Now and then he pauses to rise slightly on his hind legs, sniff the air, and look about. Satisfied that there is no living thing abroad except himself, he continues his slow, aimless journey.

But the bear is mistaken. He is not the only living thing moving across the ice. Some distance behind him, Kudluk, an Eskimo hunter, shatters the silence with the crack of his long, coiled whip and a shout to his team of dogs. The narrow sled on which he rides jerks forward and moves rapidly for a short distance. But the dogs see nothing ahead and soon slow again to a gentle trot.

All at once Kudluk and his team come upon the place

where the polar bear has feasted. The dogs halt and sniff hurriedly around the remains of the seal. As soon as the scent of bear reaches their nostrils, they are frantic with excitement. The hunter quickly reads the story which lies before him in the snow and he reaches back to check his rifle, lashed to the sled. Seconds later the team is off like the wind on the track of the bear. The dogs have forgotten how tired they are and need no urging. The sled bounces from one mound of ice to another, and Kudluk has to hang on tight to keep it from upsetting.

Now the dogs have spotted the bear. Kudluk sees it, also, and speaks quiet words of warning to his team. But it is too late. The bear has seen them and quickens his pace. The team gains on him. When they are only a short distance away, Kudluk shouts loudly to his dogs and brings the sled to a sudden crashing stop by swinging it into a ledge of ice. Instantly he leaps from the sled and unhitches one dog after another. Several break their traces in the excitement. In a matter of moments the bear finds his escape cut off by a circle of snarling, snapping dogs. Furious, he rises on his hind legs and begins to swing at them with his powerful paws. One blow could easily mean death, but the dogs are quicker than the bear. They rush in and out, nipping at his legs until in a blind rage he raises himself to his full height, still frantically waving his paws.

The Eskimo has crouched with his rifle behind the ledge of ice and at this moment he fires. The bear drops

Polar bear emerges from the sea onto a floating chunk of ice.

Information Office, Canadian Consulate General

forward, but he rises again to his knees. Growling and hissing, he still tries to strike the dogs, which have crowded closer and leap up at him. Again the hunter fires, and this time the huge beast drops and lies still.

Kudluk is fortunate. There will be polar-bear steaks in the cooking pot tonight. He and his family will feast until they cannot swallow another bite. There will be meat to share with his friends and neighbors and some left over for the days to come. There will also be a warm, polar-bear robe for his bed or perhaps his wife will make him a pair of new, white fur trousers.

But Kudluk is not always so lucky. Many nights he returns home hungry and empty-handed. Eskimo people spend their lives moving about in search of food. They have learned a thousand different ways in which to out-

The Tree Line is the northern limit of the forest.

American Geographical Society

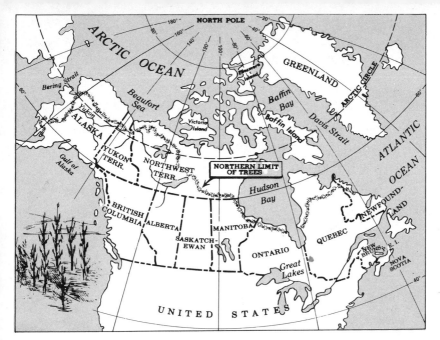

At the Tree Line the land of the Eskimos begins.

wit the snow and the ice, and to stay alive in one of the coldest and most barren lands in the world. There is scarcely an object, a living or a growing thing for which they have not found a use. Yet to an outsider the land of the Eskimos looks like a frozen white desert where no living thing could exist.

Northern Canada is a land of forests, where evergreens grow thick and tall. But the farther north the forest grows, the thinner and smaller the trees become, until at last there are almost none. Scattered here and there are only a few little sticks trying very hard to stretch upright. This is the Tree Line. Here the land of the Indian is left behind and the land of the Eskimo begins. Northward to the Pole stretches the Canadian Arctic.

It is not the coldness of the air or the violence of the wind that prevents the trees from growing. The real reason lies in the soil. To become tall and strong, a tree must have good earth in which to grow. The roots must be deep and firm, for they feed and anchor a tree. Farther and farther northward, the colder and longer the winters are. Under the snow the earth lies frozen. The summers are so short that the sun has time only to melt the snow and a thin layer of topsoil before frost comes again. This means that underneath, perhaps for several hundred feet down, the earth never has a chance to thaw out. It is permanently frozen and for this reason is known as *permafrost*. Nothing with deep roots can grow here. The low-lying plants and grasses can live because their roots are short and reach only an inch or two below the surface. The few small trees and shrubs that do manage to spring up are growing in sheltered spots where the sun's heat has been able to penetrate the earth more deeply.

In addition to the Tree Line, there is another important marking on Northern maps. This is the Arctic Circle. It encloses that part of the world which has at least one day each year when the sun does not set. Because the earth is tilted on its axis, the part surrounding the North Pole is turned toward the sun from March to September and away from the sun for the remainder of the year. North of the Arctic Circle, on June 22 the sun never sets and on December 21 it never rises.

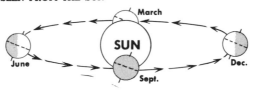

THE EARTH'S TRIP AROUND THE SUN

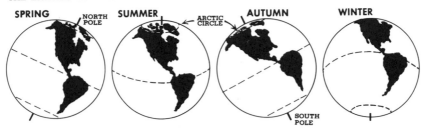

In spring and autumn the two poles are the same distance from the sun. Day and night, the world over, are about equal length. In summer the North Pole tilts toward the sun. The northern regions have long days and short nights. In winter the North Pole tilts away from the sun. Northern regions have short days, long nights.

Throughout the entire Canadian Arctic, summer days are very long. There is no real darkness. Even when the sun does disappear below the horizon for a few hours, sunset and sunrise are so close together that a pale twilight covers the land until it is bathed in sunlight once more. But it takes a great deal of sunshine to thaw all the snow and ice. In June there is still some snow on the land, and ice on the water.

On the first bare patches of ground, little plants and grasses appear. Throughout the long hours of sunshine, they grow very quickly. It is not unusual for flowers to bloom on the sunny, sheltered slope of a hill while snow still lies on the other side.

July and August are the only months of real summer. Even then patches of snow still lie on the hills, and icebergs, which once were part of the frozen sea, now float upon the water. The sun shines down warmly, but the sea wind blows coldly upon the land. Brooks and rivers run. Green growing things spring up in every place where they can sink their roots. Even the rocks have moss flowers clinging to each crevice. Every bit of vegetation is in a hurry to grow, to blossom, and to seed. Some of these plants complete their entire life cycle in a few weeks.

By the end of August, the land that was green for so short a time turns to beautiful shades or red and gold. Autumn has already come. The plants have scattered their seeds and are ready to die. Then in September, when the hills and valleys have faded to brown and gray, the snow begins to fall again. The days have grown short, the wind blows strongly, and the blue-green sea appears an inky black. Big waves froth as they beat upon the rocks.

Early in October all is once more quiet. An eerie stillness hangs over the land. The dashing waves and their seething whitecaps have been silenced and sealed under a glittering layer of ice.

For a month or more, snow falls upon a silent land while darkness gently closes in. Then, in all their fury, the winter gales come. They pound upon the ice of frozen lakes and seas, and beat the snow smooth and hard. Soon there is nothing to be seen but snow and ice and tips of the rocky hills that the wind has blown bare. The cold increases with the darkness, and so the land lies until brief summer comes again.

Nobody knows for sure when or how a race of human beings came to live in this frozen land. But today's Eskimos closely resemble a group of Asiatic people known as Mongolians. They have the same slightly slanted brown eyes, straight black hair, and flat noses. They do not grow very tall, and the men have little or no hair on their faces.

Eskimos look like Mongolians and may be of the same race.

Information Office, Canadian Consulate General

Thousands of years ago the first Eskimos may have reached the coast of Alaska from Siberia. Perhaps at that time the two were joined by land, or locked together by winter ice. Ancient people may have wandered farther and farther eastward across Siberia in search of food. The first who reached the coast of Alaska may have found the hunting so good that they decided to stay. Or perhaps they ventured too far across the spring ice with their dog teams and then found that the water had opened up behind them and they were stranded in a strange land. No one knows. But it appears that they did settle in Alaska and from there they and their descendants spread slowly across the Canadian Arctic.

Probably the first Eskimos brought nothing into the Arctic with them except the clothing they wore, the weapons they carried, and their sleds and dogs. Many must have died of cold, hunger, or sickness. Only the strongest lived, and for this reason they became a hardy race. They learned to use everything the land had to offer. They found ways to kill Arctic animals, to use their flesh for food and their skins for clothing. They learned to build shelters against the wind and cold by using whatever materials they could find. Each day they went after food at the risk of their lives. Only the cleverest hunters returned safely to their homes at night.

Today Kudluk and the other Eskimos live much as

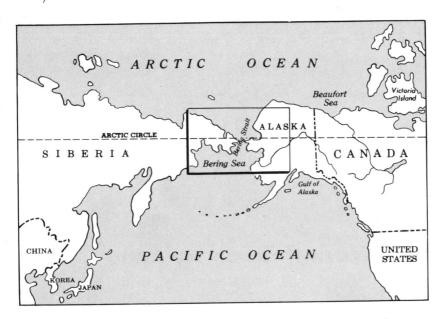

In the far north only a narrow strip of water separates Asia from North America. A land or ice bridge may once have linked them.

their ancestors did. They search for food and clothing and build their shelters against the wind and cold. But they hunt with a rifle and skin with a sharp steel knife. Civilization has brought the trading posts, and these have made available many new weapons, tools, foods, and clothing. But the people still depend upon the land for a living as did the first Eskimos who came so long ago.

2. Warmth in an Icy Land

IN FORESTED LANDS, trees supply shelter, building material, and fuel. But in the Canadian Arctic there are no trees. Rocks and hills supply the only natural shelter. Snow is the only plentiful building material.

That is why Kudluk's winter home is a house of snow. It is built on a river bank close to the frozen sea, and nearby are the igloos of his relatives and friends. Steep hills to the north shelter the Eskimo camp from winter gales.

There is little to be seen when the camp lies quiet. The igloos, almost buried, are gray, uneven mounds of snow. A high wooden rack, made of driftwood poles, supports several skin boats which have been put up for the winter. Here and there a sled lies overturned. Everywhere around the camp, dogs lie curled up in furry balls, sound asleep.

Kudluk lives in a small igloo with his pretty wife, Noona, and their baby son. It is a snug home that Kudluk himself built out of the clean, sweet-smelling snow covering the land.

The building of a snow house is a work of art. First of all, the Eskimo walks about the area where he hopes to make his home. Here and there, he thrusts a long-bladed knife into the snow. He is testing to find a spot that will yield him the best material for his work. Once he has decided, he uses long, sweeping strokes to carve out big blocks, which he places in a circle around himself. Each block requires five strokes of the knife—four in the cutting and the fifth to pry it loose. Each is cut with slanting sides so that one fits snugly against another. Round and round himself the builder places the blocks. Each new row is set to lean a little farther inward than the last, and in this way he builds a perfect dome.

A good igloo builder never once steps outside the circle until every block is cut and placed, and there is only a small hole left in the dome. All the snow used up to this point has been taken from inside the igloo so that the floor of the house is well below the surface of the snow. The builder cuts his final blocks in such a way that the floor is divided into an upper and lower level of snow. The upper level will be the sleeping platform or family bed.

The Eskimo next removes one of the blocks and crawls outside. Then he cuts a cone-shaped piece of

An igloo is built of blocks of snow carved with a long knife.

snow and with this he seals the hole in the dome. A little lower down he makes a neat hole to serve as a chimney and ventilator. A window is made by removing a snow block and fitting in a thin layer of fresh-water ice. Now, both inside and outside, the cracks between the blocks must be carefully chinked with snow. This is a job for the whole family. The wife helps with the high places while the children stuff snow in the low cracks. Often neighbors, too, are called on to help.

The main room of the house has now been roughly completed. But an Eskimo winter home may have any number of rooms, depending upon the size of the family and the ambition of the builder. Each new room is just another smaller igloo joined to one already built. The second room to be built is usually a storage place for the meat. The last and outer room is the porch, built

A second igloo room is added to the first for storing meat.

on an angle so that wind and snow will not blow directly into the igloo. It has a doorway just high enough for a man to walk through with his back bent. No Eskimo would think of crawling into an igloo on his hands and knees. He would not only get all snowy but also wear out the knees of his fur trousers. This outer porch serves as a windbreak and as a place to store guns, shovels, icepicks, and other tools that are in daily use.

Kudluk's wife is a good housekeeper and she is proud of her home. The upper level of the floor is covered with woven twig mattresses, which Noona herself made. On top of these she has spread several polar-bear and caribou skins along with some woolen blankets bought at the trading post. This platform is also used for sitting, but Noona becomes cross if anyone puts his snowy boots upon it.

The lower level is crowded with household possessions. On a shelf there are several pots, pans, and enamel mugs, a package of tea, a tin of tobacco, and a cheap alarm clock. On the floor are sealskin bags full of clothing, guns, fish nets, traps, and sewing equipment. Near the doorway stands a wooden stick with a neatly carved handle. Kudluk and Noona use it to beat the snow from their clothing each time they enter the igloo. Beside it sits a brown-stained tin can which they keep for the convenience of their tobacco-chewing visitors.

By far the most important utensil in the igloo is the *koodlik*, the oil lamp that supplies both heat and light.

Women tend the koodlik, which supplies light and heat.

The koodlik was designed thousands of years ago by the early Eskimos, yet it is still the best and most popular way of heating a snow house.

A koodlik is made from a hollowed piece of soft stone. The hollow is filled with oil from animal fat. A wick of fine moss is carefully laid along one edge of the koodlik, and it draws up oil. When the wick is lighted, it burns with a strong, steady flame. It keeps a snow house at just the right temperature—comfortably warm, but not hot enough to melt the walls. Day or night, the flame is never allowed to go out, and the igloo keeps an even temperature.

The koodlik is also used for cooking. A greasy, black-bottomed pot, in which something always seems to be simmering, hangs over the flame.

Bowl of the koodlik is carved out of soft soapstone.

National Film Board of Canada

Noona's place in the igloo is close to this fire. There she sits sewing, cooking, or caring for her baby, and at the same time keeping a careful watch over the flame. She trims the wick, refills the hollow with oil, and is happy because hers is an important task and she is doing it well.

When Kudluk goes on a winter's dog-team journey, he takes along a primus stove that he bought at the trading post. It looks and works somewhat like the old-fashioned lamp. Kerosene is used for fuel. Almost every Eskimo family owns one of these little stoves. It gives a quick, strong heat which can boil a kettle or warm a temporary igloo along the trail.

Kudluk and Noona do not live in the same snow house all winter. A new igloo is a warm igloo, but after a while the wind blows the walls thin and the chinks between the blocks begin to loosen. A thin layer of ice may form on the inside walls. When this happens Kudluk builds a new house nearby and the old one is abandoned. Noona never needs to clean house because when her home becomes dirty it is usually time to move.

With the coming of spring, an Eskimo camp may be almost buried beneath the snow. Neighbors will have built connecting tunnels under the drifts between their homes so that they can visit back and forth without going outdoors. But as the sun rises higher in the sky and shines for longer periods each day, the snow banks turn gray and begin to sink. This is a miserable time for all the People of the Snow. Their igloos become damp and cold. Water drips from the walls and ceilings. The ice window melts and the cool spring winds blow in. The family tries to stop the drips by dabbing them with bits of soft snow, and they patch up the window with pieces of sealskin. But it is of little use. A spring igloo is a sad sight.

Everyone watches eagerly for the first bare patches of ground. Then the *topiks*, or Eskimo tents, begin to go up. Spring moving is a happy event. When all the family possessions have been dragged out of the old, sagging igloo, the children take over. Laughing and shouting, they run back to climb over it and jump up and down until it lies in crumbled ruins. The mothers and fathers watch good-naturedly. The breaking-up of the last igloo marks the end of the long dark winter.

Everyone loves the warm spring and summer sunshine. The old people now sit out beside the tents to doze and dream, and soak up the warmth. The small children run about and play all day long. When they are tired, they often curl up to nap on a sheltered ledge of rock or sunny hillside. Both young and old work and play out of doors as much as possible during the short season of warm weather.

The summer home of Kudluk and Noona is made of canvas. Kudluk bought the canvas at the trading post and Noona, with the help of her friends, made the tent. It is small and low so that the wind cannot easily blow

Summer tent is built in shelter of rocks that shield it from wind.

it over. When the canvas was new, it was a shining white, but now it has become a dirty gray. There is a rough wooden door in front and a hole in the roof where a piece of rusty stovepipe sticks through.

When an Eskimo woman wishes to make a new tent, she chooses a warm dry day for the task. First she unrolls the new canvas on the grass. Next she carefully cuts out the pieces. Then she gets out her little portable sewing machine and, sitting cross-legged, begins to sew the long seams. Many of her neighbors come over with their own machines. Each takes up a piece of the work and helps. Soon everyone is laughing and gossiping as the needles fly up and down and the little wheels spin around and around. It is a real party, complete with a kettle of tea.

Because almost every family makes its own summer home, the tents are all different shapes and sizes. The canvas is supported by wooden frames. Ropes or pieces of skin line are attached to the top of the tent walls, and these are fastened to small rocks placed in a circle round about. The sites of old Eskimo summer camps can easily be recognized by the rings of rocks left behind.

Before traders came into the land, the Eskimos made their tents of seal or caribou skins. The women used needles made of bone and animal sinew thread to sew the skins together. The making of such a tent was a long and tiresome task. Today canvas is widely used, and there are very few of the old skin tents left.

The inside of a tent is laid out in much the same way as an igloo. The sleeping platform is raised with earth or wood. Heat is most often supplied by a little home-made tin stove that burns moss and twigs. Around the canvas walls are piled guns, knives, meat, fish, boxes, and bales. Damp clothing hangs drying on the tent poles. When the summer home becomes dirty the family moves it to a fresh piece of ground.

All summer the Eskimos are happy living in tents. But too soon autumn comes again. The weather grows colder and icy winds blow off the sea. The tents become drafty, and the stoves begin to smoke. Rain and sleet

The inside of a tent is arranged much like the inside of an igloo.

beat down on the gray tents, gray rocks, and grayer seas. This is another miserable season. A cold tent is even more unpleasant than a damp igloo.

As soon as the snow begins to fall the people start banking up the canvas walls, but it is often many weeks before an igloo can be built. Meanwhile they bank their tents higher and higher. It is a happy day when one of the hunters of the camp pulls his long-bladed knife out of the snow and announces that at last an igloo can be built.

Without complaint Eskimos adapt themselves to each season as it comes. They enjoy to the utmost the pleasant days. The miserable ones, which they can do nothing about, they try to ignore. Long ago the People of the Snow learned that there is no use fighting something that cannot be changed. While the winter winds howl outside, they huddle in their cozy igloos and are thankful for many things.

Without the snow they would have no sheltering walls to shut out the storms. They also know that without the warmth and light from the burning oil in the koodlik their igloos would be cold and dark. So they are grateful for the animals of the icy sea and snowy land. For these provide them not only with fat for fuel oil, but with food and clothing as well.

In summer icebergs float on water, though color touches the land.

Royal Canadian Naval photo

3. Hunters and the Hunted

NORTHERN LIGHTS shimmer across the frosty sky. They glow, fade, and reappear to shatter the darkness with the speed and brilliance of a thousand silver arrows. Far below, the Arctic winter world lies silent and cold. Snow covers the frozen lakes, the rocky hills, and the grassy plains. Mounds of ice catch and reflect the ever-changing pattern of the sky. In the valleys, flickering shadows play across the snow. Only the sharp crack-lings of frost echo from rock to rock across the eerie stillness of the land.

A group of dark shapes files across the barren white-ness of the plain. Sometimes they break ranks to spread across the snow, but they always return to continue their slow steady journey. Some distance behind, and to one side of the group, a smaller shape slinks in the shadows of the hills. Stealthily it follows the progress of the group, never venturing out into the open, yet never allowing it to be lost from sight.

A small herd of hungry caribou who have chosen to spend the winter on the barren lands are moving about in search of a new feeding ground. They are seeking a spot where the snow is soft and shallow so that they can get at the grasses beneath. Their dreaded enemy, the Arctic wolf, like some evil monster, lurks behind. The shaggy white-coated beast is also hungry. He will stay near the herd for many nights and days until one of the unfortunate animals, weakened by hunger and exhaustion, lags behind. Then, alone with his victim, the wolf will strike. With one of its numbers missing, never to return, the herd moves on. The wolf feeds greedily. Then with his hunger temporarily satisfied he goes off into the hills to sleep.

Almost every animal and bird of the Canadian Arctic is a hunter and is itself hunted. The desperate search for food is never ending. Death follows in the footsteps of every living thing. The little lemming scurries as the owl swoops overhead, the wolf stalks the hungry caribou, and the polar bear watches beside the seal hole. But the greatest enemy of them all is man.

The Eskimo is a wily hunter. He has learned to be as cunning as the wild things he hunts. He knows their ways, where they make their homes, and on what they feed. The smallest tracks on the snow tell him a story.

Every escape trick known to the animals is also known to him.

The ways of the wild have been handed down from generation to generation. Among Eskimos, hunting is not a sport. It is the only way they can obtain food and clothing. The difference between good hunting and bad hunting is the difference between life and death.

Perhaps the most surprising thing is that the first Eskimos managed to survive at all. They had only crude weapons fashioned from whatever they could find—animal bone, strips of hide, driftwood, and rock. They polished bone and chipped rock into sharp arrowheads. They searched for strong, straight pieces of driftwood. To these they lashed the arrowheads with strips of animal hide. In this way they made crude spears, which they learned to hurl with remarkable speed and accuracy.

But if a seal was speared from the edge of the ice, it might escape into the water. Then the hunter lost not only the seal but his precious weapon as well. This led the Eskimos to wonder how they could hurl a spear, yet at the same time keep hold of it so the wounded animal couldn't escape. The answer they found was a *harpoon.*

The harpoon was a different kind of spear. It had a detachable head. One end of a long length of skin line was attached to the head. The hunter would hurl the spear with his right arm. In his left hand he grasped the

Information Office, Canadian Consulate General

Polar bears provide steaks and warm clothing for lucky hunters.

other end of the long line. If his aim was good, the harpoon head lodged in the animal's flesh and the barbed edges prevented it from slipping out again. When the animal jerked to get away, the harpoon head was released from the shaft. The hunter was still holding tightly to his end of the line while the other was in the animal.

A harpoon could be hurled thirty-five feet or more with enough force to kill a polar bear or walrus. But it was of little use for hunting caribou because hunters could seldom get that close to those wary animals. They needed a lighter spear that could be hurled from a greater distance. So the caribou hunter came to use a crude but powerful bow, fashioned from driftwood or bone.

Today Eskimos still use the weapons of their ancestors but almost every hunter also owns a gun and considers it a necessity. He treats it with care, and he teaches his sons to do the same. Small Eskimo boys learn how to handle a gun when they are seven or eight years old and soon go off alone into the hills to hunt ptarmigan. There is at least one gun in every igloo, yet hunting accidents are very rare.

Kudluk is one of the best hunters in his camp. Although he is still a young man, he has been handling a gun and harpoon for many years. The people of his coastal camp live mainly upon seal, and he spends more time hunting this animal than any other.

Seals are found in three different places: under the ice, on top of the ice, or out in the open water. Kudluk's method of hunting depends on the location of the seal.

Often, as he is traveling by sled across the snow-covered ice, his dogs will suddenly stop. They begin to sniff and paw excitedly around a certain place in the snow. Kudluk knows that they have found a seal hole.

Eskimo harpoons a seal from edge of ice in spring.

National Film Board of Canada

He jumps off the sled and marks the place on the snow. Then he drives the dogs a short distance away and orders them to lie down. When the last dog has settled, he goes back and, with his knife, scrapes away all but a thin layer of snow from the surface of the hole.

Now begins the long period of waiting. Kudluk stands silently above the hole with his harpoon raised, waiting to hear the slightest sound or see the faintest shadow beneath the snow. He may stand in this position for hours before the seal pokes up his nose for a breath of air. Then, with a powerful thrust, Kudluk drives his harpoon downward, killing the seal at once. With one hand he clings tightly to the harpoon line (he may even wind it around his leg) and with the other hand he uses his ice chisel to enlarge the hole so that he can pull the seal above the ice.

The springtime method of seal hunting is different, for then seals are most often found up on the ice sunning themselves beside their holes. Kudluk drives his team out onto the ice until he sees a seal at a distance. He leaves his dogs and, taking his gun, advances on foot. At this time of the year he usually wears a white cotton covering over his *parka* so that he cannot easily be seen. As he comes closer to the seal he watches it carefully. When it sleeps he bends over and walks very quickly. The instant it wakes, he drops to his hands and knees and does not move a muscle until the seal, having assured itself that no enemy is around, goes to sleep again.

When Kudluk gets within a few hundred yards, he no longer tries to remain unseen. He changes his tactics and pretends that he is another seal. Lying flat on the ice, he lifts his head up and down and goes through all the motions of a seal as he wriggles closer. He tries to get as near as possible before he shoots. If the seal is not instantly killed, it will slip back into the hole and be lost. Sometimes this method of approach may take an hour or more to accomplish. One wrong move on the part of the hunter will send the seal back into the water for the rest of the day.

Kudluk enjoys this method of hunting, although it requires a great deal of patience and he may become wet and uncomfortable from crawling through the shallow pools of water that lie on the spring ice. He gets pleasure out of matching his wits against the wits of a wild animal.

Seals in the open water are often shot from the ice floe's edge in spring. This kind of hunting is the most dangerous because the piece of ice on which the hunters are standing may break off and float out to sea. If the hunters do not have a boat with them, or if the ice does not lodge against the shore, they may die of exposure or starvation. Every spring many Eskimos are lost for weeks in this way. A few are never heard of again, but many do come ashore miles from home and finally make their way back to camp on foot.

When shot through the head, a seal, unless it is very

thin, will float. The fatter the seal the more easily it seems to be buoyed up in the water. From the edge of the ice, Kudluk first shoots the seal, then retrieves it with his harpoon. In the summer he hunts seals out in the open water from his kayak or other small boat.

Kudluk and his friends are not always successful. Kudluk may wait all day beside a seal hole and see or hear nothing because the seal has chosen that day to breathe through one of his numerous other holes. Sometimes Kudluk will spend long hours creeping up on a seal, only to have it slip back into its hole at the very last moment. There are days in summer when the water seems to be teeming with seals and there are others when no seals can be found. Kudluk and his friends have learned to be patient, to return home at night with empty sleds, and to go out cheerfully again in the morning.

Eskimos often meet polar bears on the sea ice because the bears, too, are hunting seals. When a hungry Eskimo meets a hungry polar bear, the Eskimo, armed with a rifle, is almost always the victor.

Once or twice in late winter several of the men from Kudluk's camp go inland to hunt caribou. The safest and best time to travel is just before the spring storms. Caribou steaks are delicious and Eskimos find them a pleasant change.

During the summer months, whales often enter the river's mouth close to Kudluk's camp. The sight of a

Children play aboard a large motor boat on the shore.

gleaming white back flashing on the surface of the green water can start a great deal of excitement. The men grab their guns and the women their *ulus*, or skinning knives. Everyone rushes aboard the camp's big wooden boat. The children and babies are taken along, too. It looks like the beginning of a family picnic as the boat pulls away from shore.

Terrified by the sound of the motor and the shouting of the Eskimos, the whales are easily herded into the nearest blind inlet or bay. Here as many as possible are shot before they can escape. After the shooting is over, the dead or wounded whales are harpooned and are either lifted aboard the boat with ropes, or towed ashore.

Once the men have pulled the dead whales up onto the beach, the women take over with their skinning knives. If the hunt has been very successful, much of the meat is left hidden under piles of rocks. The fat is cut into strips, dropped into barrels, and left on the shore to be rendered into oil for cooking and fuel. After the butchering comes the feasting. Then, taking some of the fresh meat with them, a very contented but tired group of Eskimos heads for home.

Hunting walrus is much more dangerous than hunting whales. Every autumn Kudluk and the other men of the camp take this same big boat and journey out to the islands where herds of the great sea monsters gather. A herd of walrus may number as many as forty or fifty. When infuriated by a group of Eskimos shooting at them from the deck of a boat, they are very dangerous indeed. A walrus, weighing a ton or more, can seriously damage a wooden boat. The angry beast rushes under the boat and tries to upset it. He tries to gash holes in it with his powerful tusks. An attack on a small open boat is even more dangerous. A walrus may hook his tusks on the sides of the boat to overturn it, while the frantic Eskimos try to beat the animal off with paddles. The air is rent with the snorting and bellowing of the walrus, the yelling of the men, and the report of rifles.

Eskimos pile rocks on seals to store them for next winter's dog food. Rocks prevent wild animals from getting at the food supply.

National Film Board of Canada

Department of National Defense

Walrus, armed with strong tusks, makes a dangerous enemy.

Kudluk and his friends may have been away from home for several weeks. Then one day, out on the dark and stormy autumn sea, the people of the camp spy the tall mast of a boat. Quickly the news spreads. The walrus hunters are coming home. The boat may be scratched and battered, and smeared with blood and grime, but if it is well loaded with walrus meat, that is all that matters. A successful walrus hunt is a good beginning for the approaching winter. The meat will be stored and used chiefly as dog food in the months ahead.

In the spring delicious fish known as the Arctic charr are speared by the Eskimos in the shallows of brooks and rivers. Summer fishing is done with homemade nets. Ugly little fish called sculpins are caught during the winter and early spring mainly by women who jig through holes and cracks in the ice with a hook and line. Sculpins are used for dog food.

Trapping is a winter occupation. When foxes are plentiful, it can be very profitable. The Eskimo sets his traps on the tops of small knolls, close to clumps of bushes, or in any other interesting-looking spot where a curious fox is liable to go.

All winter Kudluk makes regular visits to his traps, removing the foxes and resetting the traps. He takes the frozen carcasses home to Noona, who skins, stretches, and prepares the hides for the trip to the trading post. When they are ready, she rolls each one into a soft ball and tucks it into a clean cotton bag. She knows that the trader does not like dirty or greasy skins.

Kudluk likes to visit the trading post, and he enjoys himself all the more if he has many fox skins in his bag. He finds it pleasant to chat with the friendly trader and to order all kinds of fine things from the shelves. He meets Eskimos from other camps. They exchange stories about the number of foxes they have trapped and they brag a little about what they have done and what they expect to do. But the moment someone mentions seals or walrus or polar bear, then foxes are forgotten. One story of the hunt is followed quickly by another. Eskimos are hunters at heart. They have become trappers only out of convenience or necessity.

The People of the Snow have learned that in order to live they must make use of every advantage that the land offers. If fox skins, for which they themselves have no use, can be exchanged at the trading post for useful articles, then they are willing to become trappers. But their true pride and pleasure is in the hunt, for it is by hunting that they obtain the best and greatest part of all their family's food and clothing.

4. After the Hunt

WITHOUT THE GREAT wild beasts that roamed the land, the early Eskimos could not have survived. Today animals are still the Eskimos' main source of food and clothing. Nature provides the Arctic beasts with coats of heavy fur so that they may survive the violent winds and extreme cold. The same fur will keep a human being warm. The flesh of these animals is the best of food because it contains all the vitamins necessary for survival. The animal fat provides an outer warmth when burned in the koodlik. And when eaten, it provides an inner warmth to heat the body. Even with all the products on the shelves of trading posts, there is no material or food of greater value to Eskimos than the natural products of their land.

The two skins most widely used for clothing are

Information Office, Canadian Consulate General

Eskimos dress in the skins abundant in the region where they live.

caribou and seal. In parts of the Arctic where seals are in abundance, the Eskimos clothe themselves almost completely in sealskins. The adult harbor seal, the most common variety, is a silver-gray mottled with white. The skin itself is strong and windproof. The hair is short, thick, and smooth. Sealskin makes good work clothing and sturdy boots.

Soft caribou skin is very warm. The hair is long, silky, and pleasant to the touch. Its pretty shades of brown and white make up into parkas, trousers, boot tops, and mitts. Eskimos like to wear caribou clothing in the very cold weather. Because it is light in weight, as well as windproof and warm, caribou makes ideal wear for traveling. Sometimes two parkas are worn at the same time, the inner one with the fur turned toward the body and the outer one with the fur turned out.

Caribou socks with the fur turned in are often worn inside the outer boots. These absorb perspiration and keep the feet from becoming clammy and chilled.

After the early Eskimos had hunted, killed, and skinned the animals, they had to find a way to join the skins and make garments. The task of stretching, drying, cutting and sewing these skins was given to their wives. From animal bone the women fashioned needles, and threaded them with dried lengths of animal sinew. With bone knives they cut the skins into pattern pieces. They chewed the edges to make them soft so that the needles could pierce the skin.

The women learned to retain a pattern in their minds and to make a garment to fit someone merely by look-

Sealskin stretched and drying on rack will be made into boots.

National Film Board of Canada

ing at him. Today Eskimo women have still not lost this art. They rarely measure anything, yet they produce some of the most comfortable and best-fitting garments in the world.

Kudluk's wife Noona is a fine sewer. It is very important to an Eskimo hunter that his wife be able to sew well, for his life depends on it. Poorly sewn garments will let in the cold and he may freeze to death. It is more important that an Eskimo girl be taught to sew than to cook. Noona's mother first began to teach her how to hold a needle when she was five years old. Now she stitches quickly and evenly, and there is not a day in her life that she does not do some type of sewing.

Eskimo women no longer sew with needles made of bone. They buy steel needles at the trading posts because these are stronger and sharper. In her sealskin sewing bag, Noona has many different sizes of steel needles, but the thimble which she slips on her finger is made of bone. She sews her skin garments with animal sinew as her ancestors did long ago, but if she runs out of sinew she asks Kudluk to get her a few balls of strong, white twine at the trading post.

Skin clothing requires a great deal of care. Each night, when Kudluk comes home to the igloo, Noona carefully removes every speck of snow from his boots and outer garments. Using her teeth and fingers, she softens any spots that have hardened. Then she searches

Parka has openings only for head and arms.

for tiny tears in the skin. These she sews at once before they become larger. After she is satisfied that his clothing is once more in perfect condition, she hangs it on high racks ready for the following day's wear. If Kudluk plans to be away from home for more than one or two days, he takes Noona with him to look after his clothes.

Kudluk's most important outer garment is his parka. It looks like a long tunic with an attached hood. An Eskimo parka has no front opening. Kudluk gets into his by first putting his arms into the armholes and then wriggling the whole thing over his head. In a land where cold winds sweep across the snow, outer garments must have as few openings as possible. Kudluk also wears trousers, knee-high boots, and mitts.

Noona's own parka is cut a little differently. It is short at either side with a long apron hanging down behind and a shorter apron in front. Eskimo women do

Information Office, Canadian Consulate General

Women's parkas are cut
longer in front and back.
This one is made of duffle cloth.

a great deal of sitting on the snow or ice when they are out of doors. They crouch on the snow to prepare a wayside meal while traveling, or on the ice beside a fishing hole in winter. The long apron behind protects them from the cold. The hood of Noona's parka is wide, and it has a big inside pouch just over her shoulders. The pouch makes a warm and comfortable nest for the baby. Noona wears trousers and knee-high boots like her husband, but over the trousers she wears a thin skirt made of gay cotton print.

Noona makes her family's clothing from sealskin, caribou skin, or duffle cloth. Eskimos are very fond of the trader's duffle cloth, especially for summer wear. It is a soft, white, woolen material, rather like blanket cloth. Almost everything can be made out of it, except boots. It is not windproof or as warm as animal skin, but it is light, comfortable, and washes easily.

Kudluk's summer boots must be very strong so they will not be cut to shreds by the sharp rocks and stones that cover the land. They must also be waterproof so that he can wade into the water to pull his boat ashore or to get a wild fowl that he has shot. For this reason Noona makes them of sealskin from which she scrapes the hair but not the black, waterproof, outer coating of the skin. She sews the boot seams together in such a way that no water can leak through. Sometimes she uses very tough walrus or whale skins for soles.

Kudluk's winter boots are made of the same material, but Noona leaves the hair on the boot tops so that they will be warmer. For the foot covering and soles, she scrapes away both the hair and the black outer layer. This leaves the skin softer and whiter. It is not as water-proof, but it does not freeze as easily.

A baby travels in the warm pouch of his mother's parka.

National Film Board of Canada

Noona makes her own boots in the same way, except that she adds a little more decoration around the tops. Eskimo garments must be practical and perfectly suited to the climate in which they live, but the women who do the sewing like them to be pretty as well. They often sew long strips of white or light-colored fur into the garments so that a pattern is created. They like to decorate their own parkas with tiny glass beads, bright wool or braid, little bone ornaments, or dangling rows of animal teeth.

Eskimo children are dressed exactly like their parents. Little girls even have a tiny pouch in the back of their parka hoods where they can carry a sealskin doll. Noona's small son, as yet, needs only a few clothes because he spends most of his time in her hood, where he is kept warm by the heat from his mother's body. He has a few little rabbit-skin shirts with the fur turned in, which he sometimes wears. As soon as her baby is old enough to walk around by himself, Noona will make him an outfit of clothing exactly like his father's.

Clothing and food are closely related in the life of an Eskimo. The same animal that provides the hunter with tops for his new boots supplies him with his dinner. An Eskimo dressed in sealskins eats mostly seal meat, and caribou meat is probably the chief food of the hunter who is clothed from head to toe in caribou skins. Eskimos do not choose that type of animal skin in which they wish to clothe themselves or the meat that they like best to eat. As in all things, they must take what their land provides.

There are many strange beliefs concerning the Eskimo people, and one of these is that they prefer to eat their meat raw. This is not true. Eskimos will eat slices of frozen raw meat if they are very hungry and they have no way of cooking it. Sometimes, especially while traveling, they will eat pieces of frozen raw fish. But if there is a fire, a cooking pot, and a little water handy they would much rather make a stew.

Noona's cooking equipment is very simple. She has two large open kettles, one for boiling tea and the other for boiling meat, fish, or fowl. Boiling is the Eskimo's favorite way of cooking. In Kudluk's igloo, there is most often seal meat in the pot which hangs from a hook over the flame of the koodlik. It is good food and gives the family bright eyes and fat, rosy cheeks. Sometimes there is polar bear or rabbit in the pot, and once in a while a piece of caribou meat. In the summer they often eat whale meat and many kinds of fish and fowl.

When the meat kettle is taken off the hook, the tea kettle goes on. All Eskimos are very fond of tea from the trading post. Even the babies cry for tea. Noona piles the kettle high with snow and when this melts she throws in a large handful of tea and allows the mixture to boil vigorously. Then she removes the kettle of black brew and adds more snow until it cools to the proper temperature for drinking. She and Kudluk and their guests gather around and dip big enamel mugs into the kettle. They drink one cupful after another until there is nothing left but the tea leaves in the bottom. Often they reach in with their fingers and eat the leaves as well.

In the early summer, birds' eggs form part of their meals. They also eat the roots, stems, or leaves of various plants. In autumn, when the tiny Arctic blueberries and cranberries are ripe, Noona and her friends go walking over the hills in search of them.

The early Eskimos depended entirely upon the land to supply them with food. In the winter months when the animals became scarce many families starved to death. Today this rarely happens. The Eskimo has come to accept the trading post as a natural part of his surroundings. He depends on it to supply him with part of his diet. Flour, tea, baking powder, and sugar can now be found in almost every igloo. Today, when the natural food of the land is scarce, Eskimos buy canned and packaged foods on which they live until fresh meat is once more available. They like this food from the trading post, but they soon tire of it and long for a feast of seal or caribou.

Eskimos do not eat three times a day at special hours. They eat when they are hungry or when they have time, which is usually after the hunt.

Mealtime in Kudluk's igloo may be at any hour of the day or night. Noona sets the cooking pot on the floor and Kudluk and their guests gather around. Eskimos always seem to have guests because everything they have is shared. The men dip their fingers in first and choose the best pieces of meat. The women and children eat what is left. This is not considered impolite.

Eskimo trades skins at trading post for food supplies.

National Film Board of Canada

Eskimos believe that the men who brought home the meat should have first choice.

Everyone has a small sharp knife. Instead of biting off small pieces of meat, the Eskimo puts one end of the large piece in his mouth. Then he cuts off small, bite-size pieces by rapidly flipping the knife blade down in front of his nose. To anyone who is not an Eskimo, this is a terrifying process to watch. It appears that at any moment the Eskimo's nose will drop into the cooking pot. But that never happens.

After a successful hunt Eskimos stuff themselves until they cannot hold another morsel. The dogs do the same and are sometimes found lying on their backs unable to get up. For the next three or four days everyone may eat very little. An Eskimo reasons that his life is so dangerous and uncertain that he may not be alive to enjoy the food he puts aside for the following day. He eats every morsel that he can and has no worry for the morrow.

Feasting is one of the greatest enjoyments of the People of the Snow. They feast, they sleep, and then they hunt again. All the while, the wildlife is moving about the land, feasting, sleeping, and hunting, too. One week the Eskimos may find the animals they hunt close by. The next week they may have moved far away. They must follow them in order to live. So the Eskimos, too, travel from place to place seeking the sources of their food and clothing.

5. On the Trail

WHEN Kudluk comes out of his igloo in the morning, he looks about for his dogs. If there has been a snowfall during the night, he may not see a single one. But this does not worry him in the slightest. He digs the snow away from the dog sled, which has lain overturned so that the runners will not freeze to the snow during the night. To the front of the righted sled he lashes a small wooden box. Behind it he lays a piece of polar bear skin, and under more lashings he secures his gun and other hunting equipment. Next he gets the bundle of canvas and skin dog harnesses down from the top of a nearby pole and carefully untangles each one.

Kudluk looks at the soft white world around him. He whistles. No sound, no movement. He whistles again and follows up the whistle with a shout. Suddenly small mounds of snow all around the igloo begin to shake. A black nose pops out here and a curly tail there. Soon there is movement everywhere as the dogs flounder out of their snowy beds. Once up, each dog becomes a miniature blizzard as it shakes the soft snow from its coat. The dogs have slept comfortably all night because the snow has protected them from the wind and cold.

A great howling, yelping, and whimpering is set up as the dogs spy the harnesses over Kudluk's arm. In fact, there is almost every kind of dog sound except that of barking. Eskimo dogs cannot bark. They run about excitedly, roll on their backs, pick quarrels, and go through all sorts of antics because they are happy to be going on a journey. Kudluk grabs the first dog that is handy, shoves it between his legs and slips a harness over its head and forelegs. Then he attaches the end of the long trace to the front of the sled. One by one the dogs are hitched.

In harness, the dogs can scarcely wait to be off. They howl and strain at their traces. Kudluk shouts at them to lie down. He cracks his long skin whip to show he is serious.

When all is ready, he calls to his lead dog, who jumps to her feet. The rest of the team do the same. They put their heads down and jerk at their traces. The sled begins to move forward in leaps and bounds. Kudluk runs beside it for a little way, then jumps aboard, and they are off to the seal hunt.

On the rough land of the east, fan hitch allows each dog to pick its own path. In the west, dogs are hitched one behind the other.

Soon they are heading across the sea ice and the dogs have settled down to a steady trot. Kudluk has hitched up only six dogs this morning as he is not going far and has no heavy load. The team spreads out in the shape of a fan for some distance in front of the sled. Each dog pulls on his own trace, and each trace is a different length. The lead dog, which is usually a female, is hitched in the middle and has the longest trace so that she travels well out in front.

It is a fine morning. The snow sparkles and the sky is a dazzling blue. Ahead Kudluk can see mist rising from the open water. He talks and sings cheerfully to the dogs. They hear his voice and quicken their pace. It is the beginning of a good day's hunting.

Eskimo dogs may be of any shape, size, or color, but all have pointed ears and bushy tails that curl over their backs. Puppies, with their beady eyes and long silken coats, quickly become the children's pets. The boys hitch them up to small toy sleds and the girls pretend they are babies and carry them around in their hoods. When the mother dog is a member of the team the puppies must be carried in a box on the sled. Each time the travelers stop to rest and boil a kettle of tea, the mother dog feeds her pups. All summer the puppies run and play. When winter comes again the spring puppies run loose beside the team. By the time they are a year old they have been put in harness and their carefree days are over.

The life of an Eskimo dog is a hard one. For one meal of frozen meat or fish a day he will pull his heart out for his master. At night he will sleep untethered close to the igloo, to await the harness in the morning. An Eskimo's most valuable possession is his dog.

The dog sled is simply constructed. Wooden cross-bars are lashed with skin line to a pair of strong wooden runners. Nails or screws are not used because they would be shaken loose by the jolting. The early Eskimos tipped the runners with bone because this was the only suitable material they had. Today, Eskimos use steel shoeing which they buy at the trading post. A layer of mud is spread over the steel and then a layer of ice is smoothed over the mud. Ice does not stick if applied directly to steel. The important task of icing the sled must be done often. Several times during a long journey the driver will stop his team, overturn the sled, dip a small piece of bearskin into a kettle of water he has heated, and quickly rub the skin up and down each runner. The water instantly freezes to a smooth gloss. Then the sled will slip easily over the snow and ice.

An Eskimo may travel by dog team half a mile to his fishing holes or a hundred miles to the nearest trading post. The sled he uses may vary in length from six to twenty-five feet, depending on the distance he is to travel and the size of the load he carries.

There are no mileposts dotting the barren white expanses of the Canadian Arctic. Eskimos speak of distances in "sleeps." A "sleep" is one day's travel and one night's rest in a little igloo which the traveler hastily builds where he stops in the evening. Three "sleeps" means that the Eskimo must sleep three times before he reaches his destination. There are no special roads or trails. Eskimos are guided by the coast line, by stone cairns they build on the top of high hills, and by their own almost perfect sense of direction. An Eskimo is rarely lost. If a bad storm blows up he stops, unhitches

Light, silent kayak is propelled with a double-bladed paddle.

his dogs, pulls out his snow knife, builds an igloo, and crawls inside to wait for better weather.

Dog team is the only form of transportation from October to June. Even when the snow has left the land, travel continues for as long as possible on the sea ice. This is the season when the dogs must wear little seal-skin boots to protect their feet against the sharp splinters of ice left on the melted surface. As the days grow warmer, shallow pools of water cover the ice. The dogs are forced to wade through the chill water with the sled swishing along behind. Eskimos do not give up their dog teams until the last possible moment.

Kudluk's dogs do not work during the summer months. They are allowed to run loose and go off hunting over the hills. When his dogs are idle Kudluk feeds them only about once a week. The rest of the time they must search for their own food.

As soon as the ice begins to break up, kayaks appear on the first open patches of water. A *kayak* is a light, one-man boat designed for hunting upon the water. The frame is made of wood which has been steamed until it will bend without breaking. Seal or walrus skin is stretched over the frame and sewn together with waterproof seams. Except for a small opening on top, the kayak is completely covered over. The hunter fits his body into the opening. He grasps the middle part of the long, double-bladed paddle in both hands. Gracefully he dips the paddle first on one side and then on the other, propelling the craft smoothly and quickly through the water.

The kayak's silence in the water makes it an ideal craft for summer hunting. The hunter can slip up on a seal almost before it has time to become aware of his presence. Because the kayak is light in weight it can be carried quickly and easily from place to place.

The early Eskimos had another somewhat similar type of boat which they called the *umiak*. It was built like a kayak but was larger, flatter, and open-topped. It was used to carry women, children, and household goods from one camp to another.

Today the old-fashioned umiaks are almost unknown. They have been replaced by sturdy wooden boats from the trading posts. These last longer and serve the purpose much better. Wooden canoes, flat-bottomed skiffs, and large whaleboats equipped with a single sail are now commonly seen about Eskimo camps.

The people of Kudluk's camp are the proud owners of a peterhead boat. A *peterhead boat* is a stout, seaworthy craft about forty feet long. It has a small cabin below deck in front and another cabin that encloses the gasoline-powered motor near the back. There is a tall mast and a sail that can be used when needed. A peterhead must have a crew of not less than two men— one to run the engine and one to steer. These boats are used for moving whole camps from place to place and are especially useful for whale and walrus hunting.

The peterheads got their unusual name because they were first designed and made in Peterhead, Scotland.

There is no one family in Kudluk's camp that could afford to buy such an expensive boat. Several winters ago, when the white foxes were plentiful, all the hunters of the camp got together and decided to buy one among them. They could not pay for it in one winter, but the trader said this did not matter because he knew they were good trappers and honest people. That summer he let them take the beautiful big boat home to their camp. Each year they brought more and more fox skins to the trading post, and the debt grew smaller and smaller. Now the peterhead is all paid for and the people are very pleased.

Almost all forms of summer transportation are on the water, but Eskimos also do a great deal of walking overland. The men often carry heavy loads strapped to their backs. The women sometimes carry household supplies between them on a wooden litter.

The people of Kudluk's camp do not live in the same place all year round. Hunger drives them to follow the movements of the fish and game. In winter they like to live in a sheltered spot close to the sea ice where seals are plentiful. Often in the spring they will all move far out onto the ice itself. Later on they may move to the shore of an inland lake and spend some time fishing through the ice. The main summer camp is usually on an island at the river's mouth. This is not only a good base for seal and whale hunting but also a fine location for catching the fish that go down to the sea in summer and up the river again in the autumn.

Everyone enjoys moving from place to place. There are no goodbyes said, for no one is left behind. Living, hunting, and even traveling together is all part of the Eskimo way of life.

In summer, when the sea ice melts, Eskimos must walk overland.

National Film Board of Canada

6. Way of Life

THE WISEST MAN in all of Kudluk's camp is an old hunter by the name of Anoutak. His face is lined and weather-beaten from the storms of many winters, and there is a deep scar across his cheek where a polar bear once slashed him. The straight black hair that straggles down over his forehead is touched with gray. His back is bent from long hours of stooping over seal holes, but his eyes are still bright and his aim is steady.

Everyone in the camp likes and respects Anoutak. Even the young men agree that he is still the cleverest hunter of them all. They ask his advice on many matters and they always do as he suggests. No one would think of making an important decision without first consulting Anoutak. He is accepted by all as the leader of the camp.

Every Eskimo camp has a man like Anoutak, a hunter who is looked up to and depended on by the others. An Eskimo camp usually has fifteen to thirty people. A single Eskimo family could not survive alone, for if the hunter brought home no food day after day his family would starve. In a camp where there are a number of hunters, at least a few are likely to be successful. Their meat is then divided among all the families. The next day, if another few hunters have good luck, it is their turn to share with the others. In this way, all are able to exist. If one hunter is injured or sick, then the others care for his family until he is well again.

The People of the Snow enjoy company. They are fond of their families and friends, and they love to get together so they can chat and exchange stories. If they have to go away for any length of time, they quickly become homesick. They build their igloos close together so that even on the stormiest day they can visit back and forth. This sociability is another reason why they live in groups.

Eskimo winter camps are scattered along the coast, sometimes as far as fifty miles apart. The people of different camps are usually on friendly terms. Whenever they meet, whether on the sea or the snowy trail, they like to stop and exchange news over a mug of tea. A camp that is hungry can ask for food from a camp that has plenty, and the request is never refused. Only by helping one another have the Eskimo people managed to

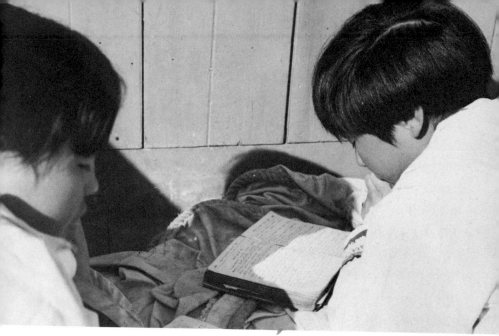

Whether or not they go to school, all Eskimo children can read.

stay alive. A hunter who has plenty of meat today knows that next week he may be the hungry one, so he never hesitates to give.

Everyone in the camp has a special type of work to do. Not all of the men are able to go out hunting. The very old men stay at home mending nets, carving ivory and soapstone, and repairing dog harnesses. The old women who no longer can see well enough to sew work at stretching skins and softening them for sewing. The crippled boys do chores like feeding the dogs and carrying water. During the summer the girls gather moss and twigs in the hills and in the autumn they pick berries. There is a job for everyone.

No one in Kudluk's camp has ever been to school, yet all can read and write their own language. The mothers begin to teach their children when they are five or six years old.

An Eskimo mother also teaches her daughter every task that an Eskimo woman does. A baby girl is scarcely out of her mother's hood before she is set at the job of softening a small piece of leather by chewing on it. Later she is taught to beat the snow from her father's boots, to sew a tear in a garment, and to trim the wick of the koodlik.

As soon as a boy is old enough to toddle about on his own legs, his father begins his education. He takes the boy with him on short sled journeys in the winter, teaches him how to set traps, and points out the tracks of the wild animals. The boy learns to build a snow house by helping his father and by building little play-igloos for himself. He learns to stalk animals by seeing how close he can creep to a bird before it flies up from its nest in the grass. There are a thousand things an Eskimo boy learns while he plays.

Everyone, both young and old, in Kudluk's camp likes to play out of doors during the long summer days. Handball is the favorite game. The ball is made of sealskin, tightly stuffed with dried grass. There are no rules and the game may last for hours. The object is for one group of players to keep the ball away from the other group by tossing it back and forth among them. Everyone joins in—the children, Noona with her baby bouncing on her back, and even Anoutak himself. All are skillful players. It may be well past midnight, but as long as the sun still shines, the game goes on with much shouting and laughter.

Eskimos are also skillful in many other, more useful ways. They are especially clever with their hands. The people developed this talent out of necessity. Until the coming of civilization everything they possessed—cloth-

This is the kind of soapstone carving done by Eskimos.

Capital Press Service

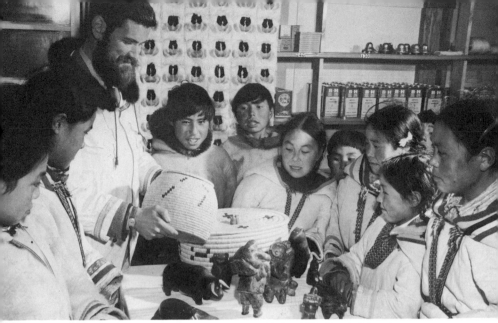

Eskimos have many other skills, including basket weaving.

ing, tools, weapons—was made by their own hands out of whatever crude materials they found available. Thus they developed both skill and patience.

Eskimo hunters long have carved small household articles, arrowheads, and tools in ivory from walrus tusks. Today they are numbered among the world's finest native craftsmen. Most of their carving is now done in soft gray soapstone, which is more plentiful than ivory. These delicately carved soapstone figures range from several inches to a foot or more in height. They are purchased from the Eskimos and highly prized by art collectors all over the world.

Weaving is another Eskimo skill. The men weave their own fishing nets from balls of twine purchased from the trading post. They make finely braided dog whips from strips of seal or walrus hide. The women use many colors of wool to weave gay parka sashes. They collect dry grasses from under the snow and during the winter months weave smooth, lidded baskets of many shapes and sizes.

Eskimo men and women, even when they are resting, like to keep their hands busy. The only time they are willing to lay down their work is when someone announces that there is going to be a feast and an entertainment.

In all of Kudluk's camp, Anoutak has the largest and finest igloo. Often, after a successful hunt, he invites everyone to come visit. All the people crowd into Anoutak's igloo—mothers, fathers, grandparents, children and babies. Eskimos dearly love their children and would never think of leaving them at home if something interesting is going on.

First comes the eating and drinking. Then, when the kettles are empty, the men light up their cigarettes and pipes. For a while all is quiet as a blue haze fills the air. Then one of the men begins to speak in a soft, singsong voice, and the entertainment has begun.

The man tells a story about something that happened a very long time ago. It is an old tale that he has heard from his father or grandfather. He has told it many times before and all the people of the camp know it almost by heart. This makes no difference to the listeners. They like a story all the better because it is familiar. When the story becomes exciting the teller jumps to his feet and begins to act out the happenings. If he tires before he reaches the end he sits down. Another man gets up and continues the story.

Sometimes they all sing together in sweet gentle voices. The songs may tell stories, too, or they may be made up of just a few rhyming lines repeated over and over. None of the words are written down, so simple songs are easiest to remember even if they do not make much sense.

The early Eskimos were a superstitious people who held in fear anything they did not understand. They could find no explanation for the northern lights and the tides that crept in and out across the beaches. So they made up stories to explain their existence. These stories told of events that were supposed to have taken place at the beginning of time. The people believed in powerful spirits who controlled the world around them. There were Seela, the goddess of the weather, Setna, the goddess of the sea animals, and many others. There were hundreds of little ways in which an Eskimo believed he could either please or displease these spirits.

The tales and taboos were passed down by word of mouth. Today almost every Eskimo in the Canadian Arctic has become a Christian, but the people have not forgotten the ancient beliefs. The old stories are still told at igloo entertainments and have become the folk-

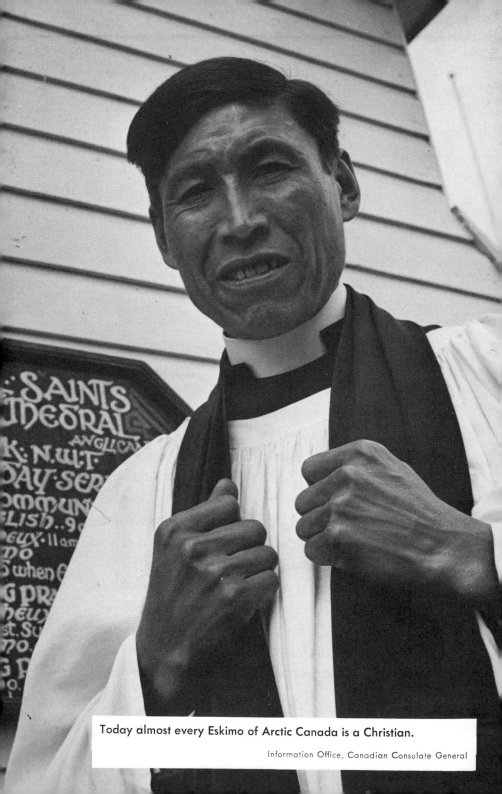

Today almost every Eskimo of Arctic Canada is a Christian.

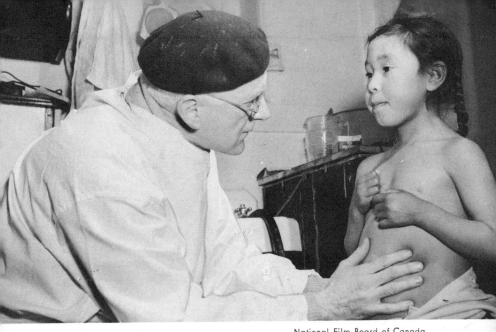

Medical care is now readily available to Eskimos in the far north.

lore of the people. Eskimo boys and girls learn these stories by heart and will someday pass them on to their own children.

The People of the Snow are combining many of the new ways of life with the old. Long ago suitable punishment for a wrongdoer was agreed upon by everyone in the camp. Today the people go to a police detachment and ask the officers there to work out the trouble. Sick persons are no longer left to die but are taken to a hospital or a nursing station in the nearest settlement. But the old way of life is much the same. The people still group together in their camps, sharing their food and their fun, as they did long before the coming of civilization.

7. The Coming of Civilization

FOR HUNDREDS OF YEARS the Canadian Eskimos and their frozen land lay unknown to the rest of the world. Civilized peoples had little or no interest in this ice-bound polar region. Sailors who ventured too far into the northern seas were frightened by fog and floating ice. They hastily turned their ships around and headed for home. They had no desire to learn of the terrors that lay beyond.

Of all the ancient seamen the Norse Vikings were the most fearless. They sailed their sturdy, high-prowed ships farther and farther from home as they fished and hunted upon the sea. Some of the more daring among them became curious to learn what lay beyond. These were the first seamen to sail across the North Atlantic

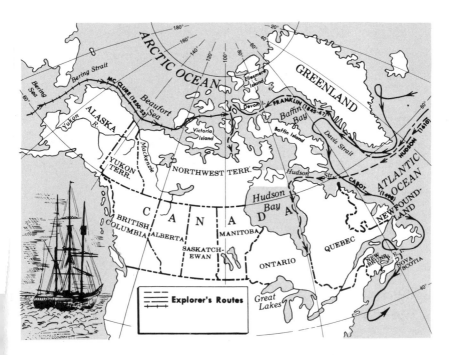

Early explorers sought a sea route through the Arctic.

Ocean. As early as the eleventh century they touched upon what is now known as Baffin Island, in the Canadian Arctic.

In Europe men slowly learned more and more about navigation. In search of rich treasure from the east, they sailed as far as China. That was a very long journey. Men began to wonder if perhaps the world was round instead of flat as everyone had always believed. If this was true, then they thought perhaps China could be reached by a sea route westward from Europe.

Columbus made his famous voyage in 1492, but he did not find China. An unknown land lay in his path.

It was the North American continent, though no one had any idea of its size.

Great interest was aroused by Columbus' exciting discovery. Seamen reasoned that the Pacific Ocean and China must lie on the other side of this new land. Expeditions attempted to sail around it to the south and to the north. A few exploration parties even tried to walk across it.

In 1576 an English seaman, Martin Frobisher, was searching for an open passage to the north when he landed on Baffin Island. Here he and his men met and quarreled with a group of native people who carried spears and were dressed in animal skins. This is one of the earliest records of a meeting between Eskimos and men from the civilized world. Later, in 1611, five crew members of Henry Hudson, another English seaman and explorer, were killed by Eskimos.

During the years that followed, many exploration parties sailed into Arctic waters. Brave Portuguese, Dutch, Norwegian, and American seamen and explorers gave their names to the rivers, bays, and mountains of the Canadian Arctic.

The sight of these strange white men and their big wooden ships must have terrified the Eskimos. The explorers had no time to make friends. It is no wonder that the Eskimos attacked in what they believed to be self-defense.

At the beginning of the nineteenth century men were

still hoping to find a northwest passage to China, but there was also a great interest in the search for the North Pole. Arctic expeditions greatly increased in number, and several exploration parties wintered their ships and made overland trips by dog sled. A little wider and more friendly contact was made with the Eskimos. It was not until 1909 that the North Pole was reached by Admiral Robert Peary of the United States Navy.

Meanwhile, in the eighteenth and nineteenth centuries, whale oil, whale bone, and baleen became of great value in the markets of the world. Lured by rich rewards for their labors, men sailed north in search of the huge whales that lived in Arctic waters. They set out in sturdy ships from Dundee, Scotland, to the Eastern Arctic, and from Seattle in the United States, to the Western Arctic.

The voyage was long and the whaling season short. Many of the whalers took lumber and supplies with them. They built whaling stations where they wintered, in order to get an early start the next summer.

These whalers were the first white men to make any lasting contact with the Eskimos. They coaxed the Eskimos to help with the whaling and taught them new and exciting ways of hunting on the sea. The whalers were also the first white men to trade with the Eskimos. They introduced them to tea, tobacco, cotton cloth, and other products of civilization.

Some of the whalers treated the Eskimos kindly, but

many others were cruel, selfish men who brought much trouble to the People. The whalers also brought with them diseases from all parts of the world. The Eskimos had learned to cope with all the dangers of their land, but their bodies had no resistance to the foreign germs. Illness spread quickly from camp to camp, and there were many deaths.

As the products of the whale decreased in value, the price of white fox skins rose higher and higher. The fur traders moved into the Far North just as the whalers were moving out.

The first Arctic fur trade post was set up by the Hudson's Bay Company in 1909. The traders quickly taught the Eskimos how to trap. The post prospered so well that the company soon set up many other trading posts from east to west across the Arctic.

The traders were unlike the whalers. They built permanent homes in the land. In the early days a trader often found himself with only the companionship of his Eskimo neighbors for a year at a time. He set about learning the language and the ways of the people around him. He learned to travel, hunt, and dress in the manner of his neighbors. There were both good and bad men among the traders, but all helped the Eskimos if they were hungry or sick. The traders realized that only strong healthy Eskimos were able to trap many foxes, and the prosperity of the posts depended on the number of skins that were collected.

Eskimos sell their carvings, which are eagerly sought, to traders.

Airplanes and helicopters have opened up the Arctic all year.

Christian missionaries came into the land about the same time as the traders. They brought new ideas to the people. Royal Canadian Mounted Police arrived to enforce the laws of the civilized world and to protect the Eskimos. Little settlements of white people began to grow up around the trading posts. The Eskimos moved closer to the settlements so they would not have so far to travel with their fox skins.

In the years before airplanes began to fly regularly in and out of the Arctic, the Canadian government could give no widespread help to the Eskimos. A ship went in each summer loaded with supplies and mail, and returned to civilization loaded with furs. The people in the settlements had little or no direct contact with the rest of the world from one summer to the next.

During the last twenty years a great change has come about in the Canadian Arctic. Air travel has opened up and brought closer to civilization this once completely isolated land. No longer is it locked away from the rest of the world for nine months each year. A journey that once took many weeks can now be made in a few hours.

Eskimos board a government ship for medical and eye check-ups.

National Film Board of Canada

"Book of Wisdom" tells where disease comes from, how it spreads, and how to take care of sick persons. It is written for Eskimos.

The coming of the airplane made it possible for the Canadian government to begin a program of widespread help to the Eskimos. Hospitals or nursing stations have been built in many of the settlements. With the help of modern radio, seriously ill or injured Eskimos can be quickly located and flown to hospitals for medical care.

In 1953 the Canadian government established a Department of Northern Affairs and National Resources. It has worked to help the Eskimos improve their marginal economy. Cooperatives to market Eskimo products have been formed, and have encouraged construction of more permanent settlements. Careful planning has immensely improved the Eskimos' situation without depriving them of their culture or reducing them to dependency.

Air travel in the Arctic has brought much-needed help to the Eskimos, but it has also brought about a new danger to the North American continent. Formerly, the great frozen Arctic lands were a natural defense against invaders from the north. No enemy would have attempted to invade the continent across the barren lands of ice and snow.

The airplane has changed all this. Enemy aircraft could now fly over "the top of the world," down across the unpopulated area of the north, and be within striking distance of Canadian and United States cities before they were spotted. This is the reason for the recent defense activities in the Far North.

There are now several large U. S. and Canadian defense bases in the Arctic. These serve as refueling points for aircraft and as weather stations. Here men are trained to live, to travel, and to defend themselves in the extreme cold.

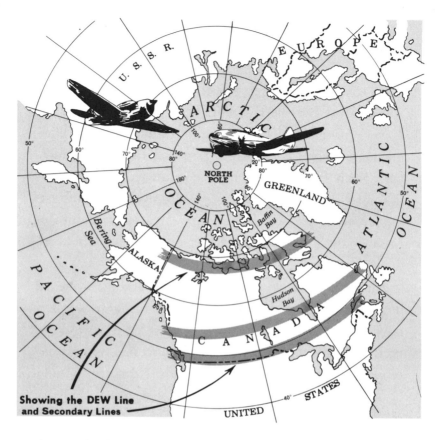

Showing the DEW Line
and Secondary Lines

Three radar lines now stretch across Canada. DEW is newest one.

A huge, invisible safety net, created by a line of radar installations, has been thrown out across the top of the continent. Any aircraft that tries to penetrate this DEW —Distant Early Warning—line is immediately detected and the news of its coming is flashed southward.

U. S. soldiers unload supplies for DEW, which protects U. S., too.

Canadian airmen study radar screens, relay information to pilots.

Eskimo men who live close to these bases and installations have been hired and trained to do many kinds of jobs. But the most important contribution of the People of the Snow toward the defense of the continent is their unequaled knowledge of methods of survival in the Arctic. Military authorities realize that there is much to be learned from the Eskimos. Their manner of dress is being copied in the making of Arctic military uniforms. Eskimo instructors teach airmen how to build snow shelters and care for themselves until help arrives, in the event that their aircraft should be forced down in the Arctic wilderness. They also serve as guides.

In the beginning, the People of the Snow were con-

Servicemen in Arctic have learned to dress as Eskimos do.

National Defense photo

Eskimos teach airmen how to build emergency shelters in snow.

fused by all the new things that came so suddenly into their lives. They made many mistakes. At the trading posts they bought articles for which they had no use and foods which were not good for them. Excited with their first guns, they shot more animals than they could eat, and much meat was wasted. Herds of walrus and caribou were so dangerously thinned out that the government had to protect the people from their own thoughtlessness by enforcing laws that permitted these animals to be killed only at certain times.

In recent years, the Eskimos of Canada have increased both in numbers and in understanding. Diseases which at first took so many lives are now gradually being stamped out. Slowly the people are learning the best uses for the products of civilization. They are accepting those things that will improve their way of life and casting aside the others, in the true Eskimo manner of taking all that is good from the land and ignoring the useless or the harmful. They realize that many of the old, simple ways are best for them after all. And so it has come about that Kudluk and his people still live in houses of snow and watch over the seal holes as their ancestors did thousands of years ago.

Eskimos, learning new ways while retaining the old,
face future with confidence.

Index